Bygone Belford

Belford & District Local History Society

This early picture of the Wooler Road, shows the cottages just as they were beginning to be enlarged with second storeys. Behind the lamp post the corner of the Scotch Church appears and beyond it the taller building on the left was the doctor's house and surgery. The white picket fence on the right hand side is outside the Nurses Home opened in 1909, in memory of Lady Grey, the President of the Belford Nursing Association, who was killed in a tragic accident while travelling to Belford. It provided accommodation for the Belford District nurses, and a clinic where children were seen.

West Hall Farm, pictured here about 1900, was built by the then squire, John Dixon Clark, in the 1840s. It occupies a much earlier site, however. A moated manor on this site is first mentioned in 1415, and some remains of this moat are still visible to the south of the farm. During the nineteenth century, a pair of 15th century spurs and some human bones were removed from the moat.

First published in the United Kingdom, 2010, by Stenlake Publishing Ltd.
www.stenlake.co.uk
ISBN 9781840335170

The publishers regret that they cannot supply copies of any pictures featured in this book.

Further Reading

The books listed below were used by the authors during their research. None are available from Stenlake Publishing; please contact your local bookshop or reference library.

As well as back numbers of local newspapers, the sources listed below were used for research.
Census Returns for 1881, 1891, 1901 & 1911.
Kelly's Directories for the area.
Belford Survey 1970 - Belford & District Local History Society.
Survey of Belford 1995 - Belford & District Local History Society.
Aspects of Belford - Belford & District Local History Society 2008.
Northumberland County History Vol. 1 - Bateson 1893.
The Northumberland Lay Subsidy Roll of 1296 - Constance Fraser.

Acknowledgements

Thanks are due to the following for the use of pictures in this book: Audrey Atkin; Joyce Barwick; Peter Bell; Blue Bell Hotel; Sylvia Carr; Philippa Craig; Roy and Marjorie Dodds; Eileen Duncan; Erskine Memorial Church; Val Glass; John Harris; Betty Kalunian; Barbara Kennedy; Miranda Margetson; Tom Nixon; Audrey Petrie; Fiona Renner Thompson; Maureen Rutter; Mrs Tully; Barbara Twiname; Kathleen Williamson; also to Brian Rogers for preparing the pictures for publication.
The images of the organ on page 19 (81083), on page 30 (20081), on page 51 (89388), and on the back cover (82585) are kindly supplied by Beamish Museum, images copyright Beamish Museum Limited.

Thanks are also due to the many local residents who shared their memories of life in the village, and to Linda and Stuart Bankier for their help with research.

Introduction

Belford owes its origins to its position at the junction of the coastal path with a route through the hills to the west, and the availability of fresh water. It was probably used by the Anglo-Saxon kings of Northumbria on their progresses through their lands from Bamburgh to Yeavering. It is not until after the Norman Conquest, however, that Belford emerges from the shadows. The first records of individuals living at Belford are in the thirteenth century. In 1272, Walter de Huntercombe, the Lord of the Manor, was charged with assisting pirates who had seized the goods of Spanish merchants and landed with them on Holy Island; and, in 1296, Parliament's attempt to raise a tax to help pay for Edward I's war with Scotland, assessed the wealth of Belford at £57. 19s. 4d - with tax due of £5. 5s. 4 3/4 d. For much of the middle ages, Belford found itself on the front line of the border warfare between England and Scotland, and it is claimed that Well House is the only building in the village to have survived the harrying of the Scots.

By 1503, when Margaret Tudor travelled north to marry James IV of Scotland, things must have improved, as, after leaving Alnwick, she stopped in Belford to eat. Nevertheless, over the next two hundred years, Belford was hardly a centre of attraction. A visitor in 1639 described it as '*the most miserable beggarly sodden town, or town of sods, that ever was made in an afternoon of loam and sticks. In all the town not a loaf of bread, nor a quart of beer, nor a lock of hay, nor a peck of oats and little shelter for horse or man*'.

The man responsible for changing Belford's fortunes was Abraham Dixon (1689-1746), who, in 1726, bought the estate for £12,000, as part of his strategy to raise the status of his family from successful city merchants to country landowners and gentlemen. The first stage in the improvement of Belford was Dixon's purchase, in 1742, of a licence to hold a weekly market and two fairs annually at Belford, one at Whitsuntide and the other in August. This had the effect of making Belford the centre of local commerce. When Dixon died in 1746, his son, also Abraham, continued the good work. When Arthur Young visited Belford in 1770 he described the establishment of a woollen mill, a tannery, collieries and large lime kilns, with the result that the population had increased from 100 to 600 in the previous thirteen years. In addition, Dixon made use of the manorial court to enforce levels of hygiene, banning the grazing of swine in the streets and requiring the removal of muck heaps from outside the houses. Belford's status as a mail coach town, also added to its prestige, and resulted in the development of the Blue Bell Hotel as a notable coaching inn. The first half of the nineteenth century probably saw Belford at the peak of its prosperity – a flourishing market town, whose inhabitants were also employed in agriculture and coal mining in the bell pits on Belford Moor. In the 1820s, the Clark family, who succeeded the Dixons as squires, rebuilt the centre of the village with terraces of plain Georgian houses.

The extension of the railway from Newcastle to Berwick in 1849, and the building of Belford Station outside the town, marked the beginning of a gradual decline in its fortunes. Although Belford retained its post office status, largely thanks to the enterprise of the landlords of the Blue Bell who contracted to take and bring the mail from the railway station to the post office, there was now little reason for travellers to interrupt their journey at Belford, and, over time, the attractions and accessibility of larger markets at Berwick, Alnwick and Newcastle resulted in the decline of the weekly market and the fairs.

Belford's position as an estate-owned town or village lasted until 1923, and with its declining economic worth, this meant there was no pressure to modernise the village. The result, for the tenants, was that poor water supplies and sanitation were issues until well into the twentieth century. On the other hand, more than many villages, the shape and features of Belford in its heyday have been preserved. It is these features which give Belford its unique character, of which we, as a local history society, are extremely proud, and which we hope that you will appreciate as you look at these photographs from the late nineteenth and early twentieth centuries.

In 1726, the Belford estate was acquired, for the not insignificant sum of £12,000, by Abraham Dixon, a successful Newcastle merchant. It was his son, also Abraham, who chose to abandon the old manor house at West Hall, in favour of a new Palladian style mansion designed by the noted architect, James Paine. The original design shows the main, ionic pillared house flanked by two wings. The main house was completed by 1769, but in Dixon's day the wings had not yet been added.

Abraham Dixon died without direct heirs, and his great nephew, who inherited the estate, had little interest in it save as a source of funds. So, it was sold and eventually came into the hands of the Clark family in 1811. The first of the Clarks, William, employed the new up and coming north-eastern architect, John Dobson, to remodel the Hall. It was he who completed the design by adding the wings, but also moved the entrance from the front to the less imposing but more convenient, and probably less draughty, back.

The Turret shown left, was part of the original landscape design for the grounds put in place by Abraham Dixon. John Wallis, who visited the area in 1782 described the grounds thus: *'a beautiful shrubbery by a piece of water under a semicircular rocky mount, on the top of which is a neat little tower, with portholes, and at an agreeable distance to the south east, near a Chinese cottage, is an opening between two hills which lets in a prospect of the sea'*. Sadly, over the years almost all trace of these grounds has been lost.

THE HALL ENTRANCE - BELFORD

George Dixon Atkinson Clark
Squire of Belford
from 1878 to 1921

This photograph of very superior looking servants belonging to Belford Hall was taken in 1910 when the Squire was George Dixon Atkinson Clark. It shows the Butler and two Footmen, one of whom was Harold Burton, who, by the 1911 Census, had moved to the north side of the village to be Butler at Middleton Hall. From the men's uniforms it is clear that life continued to be lived in the grand style at the Hall into the twentieth century. The 1911 Census shows that, at the Hall, there were eight female servants, three male servants and a nurse at the Hall, all employed indoors.

After George Dixon Atkinson Clark's death, the estate was sold in 1923, and the village properties mainly bought by the tenants. The Hall fell on rather hard times, plans to flat it were abandoned, and, in the 1930s, turning it into a secondary school for the village was seriously discussed between the County Council and the Government. Although this idea was also dropped, in 1939 the Hall grounds did provide a games area for the children of Chillingham Road School, Newcastle, who were evacuated to Belford. The picture shows the school gathered at the front of the Hall. The gentleman at the top right is Mr. T. S. Braund, the headmaster. Later in the war the Hall was requisitioned by the army.

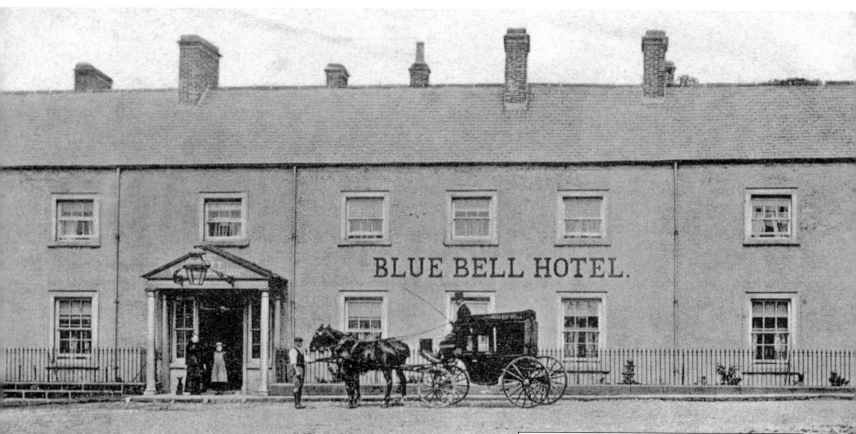

BLUE BELL HOTEL.

If the Hall was one focus of life in Belford, the Blue Bell Hotel was the other. The second Abraham Dixon is credited with building 'a commodious inn, called the Bell, for the accommodation of travellers etc.'. Among its facilities, was a splendid Assembly Room, the scene of balls, meetings and possibly even a theatre. The hotel became the stopping point for the mail coaches to and from Edinburgh, and when, with the arrival of the railway, the mail coaches ceased, the Blue Bell provided its own transport between the Market Square and the railway station, and successive landlords held the contract to transfer the mail between the station and the post office. The postcard shows the hotel and its coach when Miss Margaret Scott, who took over in 1902, was the lessee.

COACHES.

To LONDON, the *Royal Mail* (from Edinburgh) calls at the Bell Inn, every afternoon at four; goes thro' Alnwick, Morpeth, Newcastle, Durham, Darlington, Northallerton, Thirsk, York, Ferrybridge, Doncaster, Grantham, Stamford, Huntingdon and Ware.

Advert from 1822

It was not only travellers who enjoyed the hospitality of the Blue Bell. It was also a popular meeting point for locals. This photograph, thought to be taken just before the First World War, shows Jack (with pipe in the front) and Cornelius Currins (behind Jack with arms folded) and their friends with the very splendid vehicle. Jack Currins, a North Eastern Railway joiner, lived next door to the Salmon Inn. His brother Cornelius, presumably in Belford on holiday, was a boot shop manager in East Yorkshire, having trained as a shoe maker while he lived in Belford. The porch of the Blue Bell, seen here, was a later addition to the eighteenth century coaching inn, possibly added about the middle of the nineteenth century.

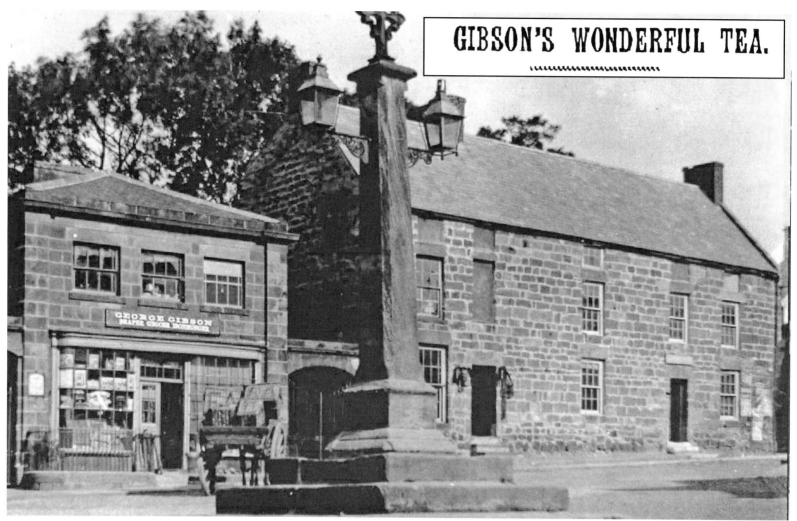

Adjacent to the Blue Bell was George Gibson's Grocery and General Store, which, by the end of the 19th century, was being run by his son David. In the early nineteenth century, the village stocks were in front of this building, and additionally served as a winning post for races held on Belford Feast day in September. George Gibson prided himself on the quality of his tea. His hand-bill of 1891 boasted that 'it removes freckles, wrinkles, and tan, arrests all tendency to grey hair'. To the right of his shop is the saddlery, thought to have been run by another of George's sons.

In 1742, the first Abraham Dixon obtained a licence to hold a weekly market and two fairs a year in Belford. Until the 1840s, local corn was sold at the market, and its price there fixed the cost of bread loaves in the village; but a whole range of general goods was also traded. Hiring fairs, at which men and women bound themselves annually for farm work took place in the market place up till the 1920s. In this picture, the water cart can be seen beside the Market Cross, and Laing's have taken over the shop from Gibson. The building behind the Cross, on the right hand corner, is the Reading Room which had been recently removed from its original premises in West Street. The tall building, dominating the right hand side of the square, is the bank, and Belford's other coaching inn, the Black Swan, is behind the little girl in the white pinafore.

This is a very early picture of the top of the Market Place as it runs into the Great North Road. Catherine Sinton, the licensee of the Black Swan, ran the inn from 1856 to 1869, taking over after her husband died 'from a fit of apoplexy, aided by intemperance'. The second block beyond it housed the Post Office for the area – Belford was a significant postal town, recorded as early as 1659.

Forty years on, little had changed, save that the licensee was now Edward Foster Nixon who took over the inn in 1895. He is thought to be the gentleman standing by the window with his children. He also kept a pair of black horses which, adorned with black plumes, were used for funerals. Not only did the Black Swan serve a clientele wealthy enough to have their own horse-drawn vehicles, but it was also an early supporter of the Cyclists' Touring Association whose badge can be seen on the wall between the windows.

John Laing's Grocers and Drapers was just below the Black Swan in the Market Place. This photograph from the late 1880s shows, it is thought, Mrs Laing outside the family shop. The two boys to the right of the delivery wagon are Joseph and Robert Clark, who went on to run a carter's business in West Street.

This pre-First World war photograph again shows Laing's shop in Belford. Little is changed, but he now also has a store in Wooler, (recorded in the 1914 Directory), and deliveries have now been motorised.

The Bank on the corner of the Neuk was the North Eastern Bank (later Bank of Liverpool, Liverpool and Martins, Martins and finally Barclays), which had served Belford from at least the 1870s. In this picture from 1920, one of the men at the door is probably the manager. In May of 1903, it was the scene of a serious accident, when the horse pulling the brewer's dray down North Bank, was killed after it took fright and bolted straight into the side of the bank building. The seriously injured driver, John Scott, was rescued from the wreckage by the Bank Agent, James Brand, and subsequently nursed back to health at the Belford Workhouse Hospital.

The Percy and Milvain Hunts have used Belford Market Place as a gathering place for the Meet since the nineteenth century, and children missing school to follow the hounds was a source of complaint for the Presbyterian Schoolmaster, Isaac Took, in 1913. This photograph, by the Berwick photographer Herriott, clearly shows the children's enthusiasm for the hunt. The four huntsmen are identified on the back of the photograph as Sanderson, Tarbit, Morkin and Greener. The 1901 census lists Charles Morkin of Waren Mill as a huntsman-groom. The Burdon-Sandersons and Tarbits were also based in and around Waren Mill.

St. Mary's Parish church owes its origins to a chapel founded by the Augustinian Canons of Nostell Priory in the twelfth century. By the end of the seventeenth century it had fallen into disrepair, and was rebuilt shortly after 1700. The second Abraham Dixon added the stone wall round the churchyard. Then, in 1825, William Clark commissioned John Dobson to improve and enlarge the church, creating in essence the building seen today. The postcard shows the improvements – chancel, vestry, additional aisle on the north side and tower. By the time this picture was taken, Dobson's pinnacles had already needed renewal, the last of the original ones being blown through the roof in a hurricane in January 1884. Immediately to the right of the church was the original seventeenth century vicarage.

Left: In 1880, Charles Robertson was appointed Vicar, a position he was to hold for 40 years – giving great service to the community. Among his innovations were a midnight carol service and carol singing round the village on Christmas Eve, soup kitchens for the poor, as well as support for a range of village activities – the Music Society, the Floral and Horticultural Society, the Literary Association and the Sewing Guild.

Above: In 1905 an appeal was launched to rebuild the church organ. Unfortunately, the repairs were disastrous, producing an instrument that was *'not in playable order, and never will be unless every part is overhauled thoroughly'*. More money was raised and the decision made to purchase a new instrument, which was installed in May 1906. Its arrival was celebrated by two organ recitals given by the Berwick organist, Mr Gauntlett. This undated photograph appears to show work being undertaken to replace the organ.

This picture of preparations for a flower festival at St. Mary's, provides a good view both of the organ and organ loft and of the 'new' Dobson aisle with the gallery above.

CLARK PLACE, BELFORD.

Opposite the church, at the entry to Clark Place, was an original eighteenth century house and dairy, although, by the time of this picture, the building had been subdivided into two houses. The higher roof line marks the beginning of the Dobson street improvements, c.1820, providing a number of superior residences for the more important employees of the estate. By the time of the photograph, the last house was the Vicarage.

THE VICARAGE BELFORD

Beyond the two Dobson Houses, lies the Vicarage. In the earlier part of the nineteenth century, this same house had served as the Manse for the Scotch Church in West Street. The figure, who can be seen through the gates, is thought to be Miss Rachel McLeish, the sister-in-law of Canon Robertson. After the death of his wife, she acted as his housekeeper, as well as teaching in the National School.

The Vicarage had large attractive grounds, ideal for fund raising events such as fetes. This photograph shows the fete organising committee for 1933. The gentleman with the cap, at the centre of the front row, is the Reverend Hull, Canon Robertson's successor, and the lady to the left of him is his wife. Those shown are:

Back row: NK; NK; Betty Rough; Jessie Dunn, nee Marshall; NK; Lilian Elliot; Jane Morton; NK.

Middle row: Mr Marshall; NK; Mrs Winship; NK; Mary Hindmarsh; Annie Clark; NK; David Rogers.

Front row: Fred Johnson; Mrs Hull; Rev. Hull; Mary Spence, nee Rogers; Mrs Elliott; Lucy Rogers; Mrs Hall.

This 1920s postcard is of the Great North Road making its way up North Bank, out of Belford. On the left, through the churchyard trees, can be seen the original Vicarage. On the bottom right hand corner, a man posts a letter at the side of the post office. The flock of sheep coming down the hill, is a reminder of Belford's Mart which opened in 1920, close to the railway station. In the nineteenth century, lamb sales in July and ewe sales in September were held in the market place.

About a third of the way up North Bank, on the left hand side, was Clark & Son, Grocers. Michael Clark opened his grocer's shop on North Bank in the mid-nineteenth century, and also was responsible for collecting butter, eggs, poultry, rabbits and game from a wide local area and marketing them in both Berwick and Newcastle. A staunch Methodist, he provided, with others, temperance refreshments at the hiring fairs in the Market Place. One of his sons, Michael, qualified as a doctor and, after having worked in the village, eventually emigrated to Alberta, Canada, where he entered politics and became a Member of the Legislative Assembly for the area of Red Deer. His other son, James, succeeded his father in the business, and also opened a second shop in the High Street.

North Bank, Belford.   10220

This postcard shows the top of North Bank about 1930. The road to the left leads down to Easington, and then to the coast. The SMT bus from Berwick begins the steep descent into Belford. Behind the postman can be seen the corner of Belford Hall's North Lodge. In December 1826, this was the scene of an attempted murder, when two guns were fired through the windows at Robert Briggs and his wife. Briggs was the gamekeeper to the Squire, William Clark. In an attempt to catch the offenders, Clark contacted the then Home Secretary, Robert Peel, for permission to offer a reward. Despite an offered reward of £50, and the promise of a pardon for the informant, no one was ever caught. Robert Briggs was not deterred by this attack, as 1838 saw him re-appointed gamekeeper by the new Lord of the Manor, William Brown Clark.

The West Hall. Belford.

This early photograph shows an Edwardian lady and her two children crossing the stile (or as it was known locally - the col) at the ford where the Belford Burn crosses the road from West Street to West Hall farm (seen in the distance). Coming off the hills near West Hall, the burn makes its way down through the village and flows into the sea at Budle Bay. In the eighteenth century, the Dixons had mill ponds dug near here to harness the water for the mill, tannery and brewery, one of the sluice gates lies just to the right of this picture.

Although normally a tranquil stream, the Burn could cause great devastation, as this picture of West Street in the great flood of 1948 shows. On the left hand side, the Maltings building emerges from the shadows.

BELFORD BREWERY.   188

Executors of the Late
Mr Wm Robson
White Swan inn Sunderland

To G. WRIGHT & CO.   Dr.,
Licensed Maltsters and Brewers.

N.B—Please stop, tap, and vent holes, and return Cask as soon as empty. Casks not returned within
two months will be charged for.

ACS. MONTHLY.   Spile the Casks through the Bung.

1880
Oct. 23   1 Kilderkin mild de 2/-   1   "   "
Nov. 9   1   do   do   "   £   1   "   "
                                        £   2   "   "

The Maltings and its brewery supplied the area with beer from the time of the Dixons until 1960 when, sadly, it burnt down on Boxing Day. In the twentieth century, the brewery also allowed the Maltings to be used for dances in the evening after the Belford Show. While Wright's had the brewery in the late nineteenth century, in more modern times it was owned by Johnson and Darling.

The Mason's Arms was established in Belford by 1825, when the landlord was William Dryden. In the later part of the nineteenth century, it was run by George Dunn, who also operated a carting business from the premises. On New Year's Eve, 1883, it was the scene of a serious stabbing incident. The *Berwick Advertiser* reported the details:

'It appears that on Monday evening about closing time, a quarrel took place with George Dunn, landlord of the Mason's Arms, and George Wood, a young man living in Belford. In the struggle between the parties, Joseph Paxton went to the assistance of the landlord, when Wood stabbed Paxton in five places in the abdomen with a knife. The police were sent for and Mr. Harkis superintendent [This was Superintendent John Harkes, stationed at Belford.]*, and his assistant, proceeded to take Wood into custody but Wood threw both Harkis and his man on the street, and went rolling over them. Wood made his escape, ran to his house in West Street, and locked the door, but coming quickly out, he was recaptured after a desperate resistance, and lodged in the police station. Dr. Burman sewed the wounds.'*

Paxton was taken to the hospital at the workhouse, where he was slowly nursed back to health. The Mason's Arms continued to operate as a public house into the 1950s, by which time it had been taken over by Vaux Breweries, who eventually closed it, but used the property as a staff annexe for the Blue Bell, which it also owned.

The front of the Maltings appears on the left hand side of this early photograph of West Street. On the right hand side is the Mason's Arms, and on the corner is the grocer's and baker's shop which, according to the 1901 census, was run by the widow, Sarah Newbegin. Beyond, the Belford Burn runs under a small curved bridge, later flattened as it was believed to contribute to flooding. The first building on the right beyond the bridge is Blue Bell Farm House. Further up on the right hand side, the hipped-roof of the Scotch Church appears behind the tall chimneys of the doctor's house.

West Street, Belford.

FRITH
BLD·16

This view of West Street, looking west, begins at the Burn. Just beyond the bridge, on both sides of the road, the entry to Tully's Stonemason's and Builder's yard is visible. It was Mr. Tully who, at the Estate sale, bought the land beyond the south side of West Street. He sold some of the land to the council for council housing and also built a new private housing development there. Previously this had been an area of fields, originally belonging to the Blue Bell and used to graze the post horses for the mail. On the right hand side, by the second telegraph pole, is the entrance to the Methodist Church, which occupied the upper floor of the building next to Tully's. The telegraph poles and telephones came to Belford in the 1920s.

This picture of approximately 1902 shows three children of Dr George Probyn Coldstream, Winifred, Nancy and Anson, in their donkey cart, outside the doctor's house in West Street. A further son, William Menzies, became a noted artist and Professor of Fine Art at the Slade School, University College, London.

This view of the upper part of West Street looks back towards the village. Davison's general store (later Nancy Ford's sweet shop) is the first building on the left; further down and set back from the road, is the Scotch Church which opened in 1777, it continued as a place of worship until about the end of the nineteenth century. After the First World War, George Dixon Atkinson Clark gave the building to the village as a War Memorial Hall. Before and during the Second World War, in this new incarnation, it served as a dance hall and cinema. In the grass outside the church one of the village wells is just visible opposite the cart. On the right hand side of the picture, where the cart is parked, is the entrance to Belford Union Workhouse, one of the smallest in the country; the flat-topped wall is the back of the stone-breaking yard. To this side of the workhouse was a smithy and the Lamb Inn.

One of the benefits of having the old church as the War Memorial Hall was that it provided a good performance space for village shows. This 1936 photograph shows the cast of 'Don Quixote' performed by the Operatic Society.

Back row: J. Brand; ? Alexander; Eva Joyce; Jackie Dunlop; Audrey Petrie; Eleanor Young; A. Fleming; R. McKay; NK; Violet Mason; Annie Aitchison.

Middle row: Johnsie Portens; Charlie Dodds; NK; Una Matthewson; NK; Mabel Pringle; Bella Turnbull; Ella Hudson; Berta McLaren; L. Joyce; Doris Cuthbert; Freda Wise.

Front row: Chrissie Temple; Mary Turnbull; Peter?; Grant Borthwick; Jack Shell; Ella Elliot; Bert Lugton; Lily Kirkup; Lilian Elliot; Adam Anderson; George Gordon.

Douglas Tully carving the 1939-45 addition to the memorial.

As for most English Villages, the First World War took a high toll in lives, both rich and poor. Fifty six officers and men were lost from Belford parish. Colonel Gerard Leather of Middleton Hall, having lost three brothers in the war, took the lead in ensuring that both a fitting War Memorial was erected, and that the Reading Room was improved to provide good British Legion facilities for those who returned. In this photograph of the dedication of the memorial on 26th March 1922. Colonel Leather is the gentleman with the medals, immediately behind the memorial. Dr James McDonald unveiled the Memorial; it was dedicated by Rev. Buffey from the Parish Church; the benediction was given by Rev. Miller from the Presbyterian Church.

Presbyterian Church, Belford.

In 1776, when the first Presbyterian church was built on West Street, opinion within the congregation was divided on the matter of who to call as their minister. This resulted in a second property being leased and converted into a Dissenting Meeting House on Nursery Lane. In 1821 the original building was replaced with a larger place of worship, which was later extended in 1875; it was this building that would eventually become Erskine United Reformed Church. In the postcard, dated 1908, the Manse is at the end of the lane, with the church to the left and the Ferguson Memorial Hall, built in 1908, occupying the foreground. The cart at the side of the Hall was probably for repair by Johnson's Builders, who had the adjacent yard. Across the lane is Belford Villa's boundary wall.

The foundation stone of the Ferguson Hall was laid in November 1904 and, in June 1905, it was opened by the Squire, George Dixon Atkinson Clark, who had given the church the perpetual lease of the land on which the hall stands. It was named after Miss Isabella Ferguson who, during her lifetime, had contributed greatly to the work of the church, and whose legacy helped build the hall.

This is a very early picture of the High Street looking north. On the right hand side the children are playing outside the Salmon Inn. The Court House building, which opened in 1867, is behind them. The railings were later removed when the Court House was extended southwards, sometime before 1881.

This view of the High Street dates from about 1906. Beyond the Salmon, the Court House Building has now been extended by an additional bay and the ornate chimney, designed by the County Surveyor, Francis Charlton. The court was on the upper floor; on the ground floor was the police house and station, including two cells, and stables at the back. Both the shadows and the children strolling across the road, suggest that the National School, which lay behind the High Street, opposite the Salmon, had closed for the afternoon.

The Currins brothers, (first and third on the left) appear again in this photograph of the Salmon Inn. John Adamson was landlord there between 1904 and 1921. The Salmon is Belford's newest pub, having been opened in 1837, the year Queen Victoria came to the throne. Unusually, by modern standards, one of the first known landlords, William Innes, was also Precentor at the Erskine Church.

In this early twentieth century photo, a range of shops are evident at the south end of the High Street. On the left hand side are the Black Bull public house, Thompson's clock shop and Elizabeth Amos's grocery shop. On the right hand side are Mabon's hardware shop, Clark's boot shop, Turnbull's the butcher, the stationers and newsagents which they also owned, and another shop belonging to the Mabons. On the corner was the house and workshop of Johnson's, the builders. The upper floor of this building, was used at times both as a drill hall and for dancing classes. In the last block of buildings on the right hand side was another butcher and Robinson's cycle, motor and implement shop. Robinson was working in Belford as early as 1880 when he is recorded as adjusting a turnip machine with the result that, in an hour, it topped and tailed as many turnips as seven women could do in half a day. Both butchers slaughtered their meat at the back of their premises, with the waste running into the Belford Burn, still remembered by some elderly residents as running red when they crossed it on their way to school.

This view of the Market Place and the top end of the east side of the High Street is thought to have been taken about 1915 when the Northumberland Fusiliers held a recruiting drive through the county. Behind the cross can be seen Macdonald's grocery and chemist store, and to the right of it the double fronted shop was the watchmaker and jeweller's run by Richard Bolton, and below it Young's the bakers.

Macdonalds, grocer's and chemist's operated in the village from about 1838 until the 1960s. Older residents remember the interior of the shop fitted with druggist's drawers and medicine bottles. This picture, shows Mr. Watson's cart from Adderstone Hall being loaded with provisions.

This postcard from about 1912 shows, behind the cross, the junction of the High Street with West Street, the road to Wooler. Immediately behind the cross, the shop beside the street lamp was Ross's. Next to it was Harbottle's grocery shop, then James Clark, draper, where his daughter, Jane, provided the millinery which is just visible in the window. James Clark was the son of Michael Clark who had the grocer's on North Bank. Below this is Hope's fruit shop, where from before 1911 to the 1950s, two generations of Mary Hopes ran the shop. In addition to fruit, the shop also sold sweets and some elderly residents recall that early in the century, the front of the bay window was filled with loose sweets and children poked their fingers through a small hole to get some out. Clearly visible are the high steps at the entrance to the shops, which survive until now.

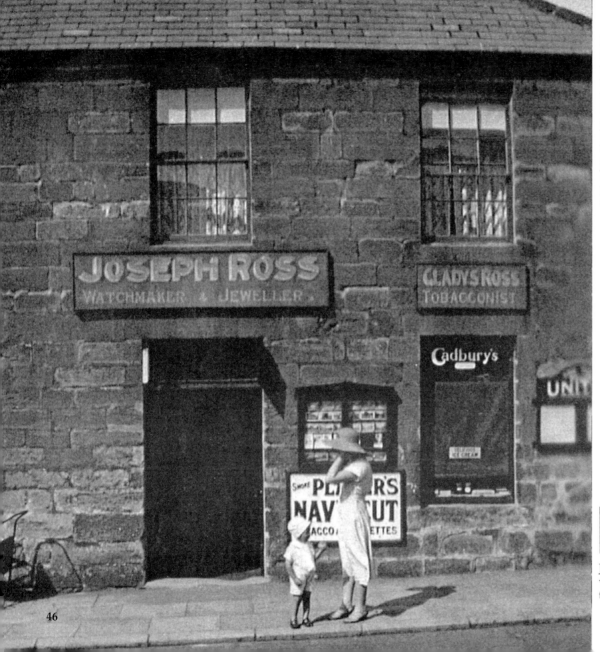

Ross's shop on the corner of the High Street is a well remembered feature. Joseph Ross was a jeweller, watch maker and repairer, who operated in the village from c.1910 until his death in a motor cycle accident in 1937. His wife, Jane, made and sold ice cream from milk delivered from Urwin's, Blue Bell Farm and Nellie Clark, West Street. Their daughter, Gladys, had a sweet shop and tobacconists at the same address. The shop was also the agent for United Bus parcel service, part of whose notice can be seen on the side of the wall.

Joseph Ross was a Company Sergeant Major with the Northumberland Fusiliers during the First World War.

The village remained essentially rural in character. This photograph shows the stack yard of the Blue Bell Farm, set in at the back of the north side of West Street. Older residents also remember it as the place where the annual travelling fair set up its roundabouts, a keenly anticipated event.

Belford. from Willie Ways.

Willie Ways, now more poshly, 'William's Way', was the lane which ran south just after the workhouse on West Street. The main entrance to the workhouse was there, and further along, a footpath led to the National School, which can be seen here – the large windowed building in the middle left of the picture, with the stile entrance just visible in the wall. Although the photograph is dated 1908 it must have been taken about 1884, as it shows the church tower before the pinnacles were replaced at the end of the century. It was this field on which the new housing was built after the sale of the estate in 1923.

This picture of the boys of the National School was taken by their headmaster, Dick Davison, somewhere about 1900 – clearly well before the days of 'health and safety'! The wall they are sitting on divided the boys' and girls' playgrounds. Davison was appointed to the school in 1900, and rapidly acquired the nickname 'Tarry' on account, it is said, of his moustache. The ornate window of the school is again visible. The school was opened in 1838, in a former non-conformist chapel on this site. The building was altered and new classrooms added in the 1860s and 1880s.

The Newcastle to Berwick railway line was opened in 1849. The company spared little expense in its building, commissioning the noted Newcastle architect, Benjamin Green, to build a series of ornate stations along the line. The building provided both station facilities and accommodation for the staff. This photograph from c.1916 also shows the gantry signal box.

This photograph, dated January 18th 1905, shows the station entrance decorated for the departure on honeymoon of Miss Constance Mary Grey (the youngest daughter of Mrs Grey, Bell's Hill, and sister of Sir Edward Grey, the local M.P.) and Mr William Cotton Curtis, of Potterells, Hertfordshire, following their marriage. The banner over the entrance reads 'Joy Be With You'. The large building behind the station is the goods shed, which once spanned two lines.

As the twentieth century progressed, the internal combustion engine came to challenge both horse power and the railway. In 1923 Thomas Herdman Nixon, the son of Edward Foster Nixon of the 'Black Swan', opened his garage at the south end of Belford. The picture shows from left to right: Thomas; Jimmy Spence; Bert Coggins; Norman Nixon.